Auditory Processing Higher-Level Language Skills

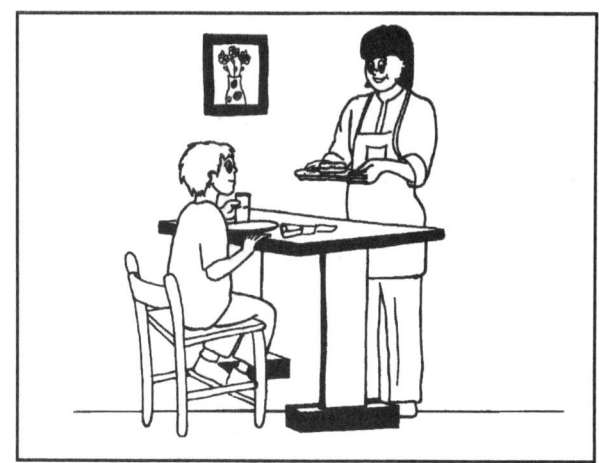

Jean Gilliam DeGaetano

Illustrations by Inky Whalen

Great Ideas for Teaching, Inc. • P.O. Box 444 • Wrightsville Beach, NC 28480-444
www.greatideasforteaching.com

Copyright 2007 Great Ideas for Teaching, Inc.
All rights reserved. Printed in the U.S.A.
Published by Great Ideas for Teaching, Inc.
P.O. Box 444, Wrightsville Beach, NC 28480

Copies of all materials may be reproduced for classroom use and homework assignments. Copies may not be produced for entire school districts, used for commercial resale, stored in a retrieval system, or transmitted in any form; electronic, mechanical, recording, etc. without the permission from the publisher.

ISBN 1-886143-57-9

Auditory Processing of Higher-Level Language Skills

By Jean Gilliam DeGaetano
Illustrations by Inky Whalen

The purpose of these higher-level language skills lessons is to help students learn to interpret events, gaining an understanding of concrete and subtle social interpretations, along with grasping the main points of each event. As additional events take place (another story), the students will learn to move on in following that new event, much as they would in going from event to event in their school day. By remembering the information and separating that information in certain higher-level language skills, reflecting back on the information in the stories should help them learn to better organize information about events in their daily lives.

While these lessons are primarily designed to improve auditory processing skills, the multiple comprehension skills that are introduced are skills that are needed in every area of learning as well as their interpretation of social language with peers. The goal of further developing comprehension skills in all of these areas is one of the main purposes of these lessons.

Observing and interpreting details in a picture is also an essential element in being successful in completing these lessons. The students should be reminded to look for clues in the pictures. The questions can be expanded by asking the students if they knew the answer by looking at the picture or by only hearing the information. While some of the answers can be determined by looking at a picture, other answers can only be found in the story's information. In easier auditory processing books, more visual clues are present than in these lessons. These lessons' pictures serve as visual reminders rather than presenting a number of clues. The main information is presented in the story information. For the strong visual-learner, the pictures may not necessarily give them answers but will help them to stay focused on the main idea of the story.

While looking at the picture, students should listen to the story about the picture. Questions are then asked that separate the story information into specific language comprehension skills, such as;

- General Information Comprehension
- Following Directions Comprehension
- Context Clues Comprehension
- Time and Spatial Details Comprehension, etc.

Being able to transfer information from skill area to skill area is difficult for some students. Practicing these tasks in auditory processing exercises before doing them in independent work helps students be more confident about doing independent work.

While these tasks may seem difficult for students with auditory processing weaknesses, learning to complete the tasks in highly structured lessons will help them learn how to separate information.

Do not consume this workbook. Use the pages as masters to make additional pages. The same pages can be used over and over again at a later date to practice other skills.

Instructor's Worksheet: Part 1

Before beginning, each student should be given the picture page that corresponds to the story page. The stories are to be read aloud to the students as they scan their picture pages.

The purpose of the pictures and the stories is to help students learn to interpret events, gaining an understanding of concrete and subtle social interpretations, along with grasping the main points of each event. As another event takes place (another story), the students will learn to move on in following that new event, much as they would in going from event to event in their school day. By remembering the information and separating that information in certain higher-level language skills, reflecting back on the information in the stories should help them learn to better organize information about events in their daily lives.

Story #1:

Carlos is riding in a horse show today. He is riding his favorite horse Pinto. Carlos is very proud that he has won lots of ribbons in small horse shows and now he hopes to win one in this large show. He also talked to Pinto about doing his very best today. He thinks Pinto understands everything he tells him because Pinto always nudges his nose against Carlos's neck after Carlos talks to him. Both Carlos and Pinto love to be in a horse show.

Story #2:

Carla is swimming in a special pool where children learn to snorkel. This pool has sharks, an octopus, dolphins, sea horses, and lots of other fish. Of course, these sea creatures are not real. They are just decorations in the water to make the pool look like the ocean. The bottom looks like sand and it has fake seaweed, coral, shells, and clams. Carla loves the octopus the best. She thinks the pool is a great place to learn to snorkel.

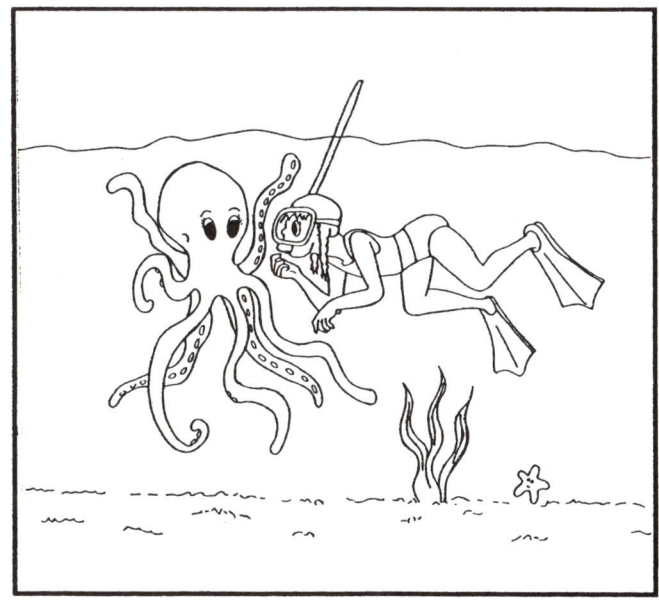

Great Ideas for Teaching, Inc.

Auditory Processing of Higher-Level Language Skills

Instructor's Worksheet: Part 2

Directions: After the stories have been read aloud by the instructor, the students should then answer the following questions for each story. The students should look at the picture pages for visual support. The first two sets of questions review the stories while the following questions break the information into higher-level language comprehension skills. Finally, the students should retell each story, giving as many details as possible.

Story #1

Story #2

Reviewing the Story About the Horse Show:

1. What was the horse's name?
2. Has Carlos won any ribbons in any horse shows? Explain.
3. Is this a small or large horse show?
4. What did Carlos tell Pinto that they had to do?
5. Does Carlos think Pinto knows what he is saying? Explain.

Reviewing the Story About Carla Learning to Snorkel:

1. What kind of lessons is Carla taking?
2. Is the octopus real? Explain.
3. Why do they have a fake octopus and dolphins in the pool? Explain.
4. What is on the bottom of the pool?
5. Can any of the fake creatures hurt them?

Separating the Main Ideas in the Stories:

1. Which story is about learning to snorkel? Which story is about a horse show?

Forming Conclusions:

1. Why does Carlos think Pinto knows what he is saying to him? Explain.
2. Does the pool where Carla takes snorkeling lessons have dangerous creatures in the water? Explain.

Separating Subtle Information:

1. In which story does the person think an animal can understand what a person is saying? Explain.
2. In which story does the person and the animal seem to love each other? Explain.
3. In which story are fake creatures used? Explain.
4. In which story does someone hope to win an award? Explain.
5. In which story is someone trying to learn a new skill? Explain.
6. In which story is there teamwork between an animal and a person? Explain.
7. In which story does someone need special equipment to breathe? Explain.
8. In which story is someone already a champion? Explain.
9. In which story is someone pretending to be in a real ocean? Explain.
10. In which story is someone wearing less clothes than she usually wears to school? Explain.

Great Ideas for Teaching, Inc.

Auditory Processing of Higher-Level Language Skills

Instructor's Worksheet: Part 2

Story #1

Story #2

Predicting What Will Happen Next:

1. What do you think will happen when the award ribbons are handed out? Explain.
2. Will Carla be afraid of the creatures when she comes for her next lesson? Explain.

Retelling the Stories:

Retell each of the stories. Tell as many interesting details as you can remember about each story.

Instructor's Worksheet: Part 1

Before beginning, each student should be given the picture page that corresponds to the story page. The stories are to be read aloud to the students as they scan their picture pages.

The purpose of the pictures and the stories is to help students learn to interpret events, gaining an understanding of concrete and subtle social interpretations, along with grasping the main points of each event. As another event takes place (another story), the students will learn to move on in following that new event, much as they would in going from event to event in their school day. By remembering the information and separating that information in certain higher-level language skills, reflecting back on the information in the stories should help them learn to better organize information about events in their daily lives.

Story #1:

Mick was so hungry this morning when he climbed out of bed. All night long he had dreamed about food and being hungry. He asked his mother if she would make him lots of food for breakfast and she did. She put the butter on the table in case he needed more on his toast. Mick's dog PJ was watching him eat. PJ was hoping Mick might decide to give him some of his food. Mick's mother noticed that PJ looked like he really wanted something to eat. Mick's mother said, "Come on, PJ, I will feed you your dog food. Maybe you were dreaming about being hungry all night, also."

Story #2: Sarah Lily

Sam was sitting on the bank of grass at the pond when Meggy and Patty came by. They were barefooted so Patty walked into the water. Meggy just stayed on the grass. Sam already had his pants rolled up and had his feet in the water. They saw that he had a plastic, water-proof box on his lap and they asked him why he had it. He took the lid off and there were four little green frogs swimming in a little water. Sam said, "I love catching them. After I play with them a little while, I put them back in the pond." The girls asked him how he kept the water in the box. Sam told them how he lined the box with a clear plastic bag. He told the girls he would make one for them and they were excited.

Great Ideas for Teaching, Inc.

Instructor's Worksheet: Part 2

Directions: After the stories have been read aloud by the instructor, the students should then answer the following questions for each story. The students should look at the picture pages for visual support. The first two sets of questions review the stories while the following questions break the information into higher-level language comprehension skills. Finally, the students should retell each story, giving as many details as possible.

Story #1

Story #2

Reviewing the Story About Mick Being so Hungry:

1. What did Mick dream about last night? Explain.
2. Was he still hungry this morning? Explain.
3. How did Mick's mom help him? Explain.
4. What did Mick's mom think PJ was trying to say?
5. How did she help PJ? Explain.

Reviewing the Story About Sam by the Pond:

1. Where was Sam?
2. Why did he have his shoes off?
3. What was in the box he was holding?
4. What did Meggy and Patty do? Explain.
5. What does Sam do after he plays with the frogs? Explain.

Separating the Main Ideas of the Stories:

1. Which story is about discovering something new? Which story is about how someone feels?

Forming Conclusions:

1. How did Mick's mom know PJ was hungry? Explain.
2. How do you know that Sam wants the frogs to be all right? Explain.

Separating Subtle Information:

1. In which story does someone ask an older person for help? Explain.
2. In which story were the people curious? Explain.
3. How did PJ let Mick and his mom know dogs can be hungry too? Explain.
4. Do you think PJ ate some of the food on the table? Explain.
5. Did Sam figure out a way for the box to hold water? Explain.
6. Does Sam plan to take the frogs home with him? Explain.
7. Will the little frogs ever get back in the pond? Explain.
8. Did all the children want to get their feet wet? Explain.
9. Did Mick even notice that PJ was begging for food? Explain.
10. Do you think the children at the pond are the same age? Explain.

Instructor's Worksheet: Part 2

Story #1

Story #2

Predicting What Will Happen Next:

1. Will Mick and PJ be hungry all morning? Explain.
2. Will Sam's box be wet and need to be thrown away? Explain.

Retelling the Stories:

Retell each of the stories. Tell as many interesting details as you can remember about each story.

Instructor's Worksheet: Part 1

Before beginning, each student should be given the picture page that corresponds to the story page. The stories are to be read aloud to the students as they scan their picture pages.

The purpose of the pictures and the stories is to help students learn to interpret events, gaining an understanding of concrete and subtle social interpretations, along with grasping the main points of each event. As another event takes place (another story), the students will learn to move on in following that new event, much as they would in going from event to event in their school day. By remembering the information and separating that information in certain higher-level language skills, reflecting back on the information in the stories should help them learn to better organize information about events in their daily lives.

Story #1: Victor and Ellie have decided to try out for the school talent show. They live next door to each other and have been playmates since they were two years old. They decided they will do a song and dance routine. Most of the kids in the neighborhood play ball, skate, etc., but Victor and Ellie have always loved music. They both take piano lessons. In addition, Victor plays the drums and Ellie takes dancing lessons. They have practiced every day for two weeks and now they are ready to try out for the talent show. Their friends asked them if they could watch and listen to them. They did and they told them they were good enough to be on television. Victor said, "Don't praise us too much or we will think we are "Hot Stuff!" Their friends laughed and said they thought they would win the talent show.

Story #2: School is almost finished for the year. Angela, Don and Mark have walked to school together for the whole year. They live in the same neighborhood. Their neighborhood is so close to school that they are walkers and do not take the school bus. This morning they talked about how much fun it had been to walk to school together all year. They all agreed that it will be great not to carry heavy backpacks for a while but that they will miss not seeing their friends for the whole summer. Don and Mark will be staying home most of the summer but Angela will be going to spend the summer at her grandparents' house. Her mother works and does not want Angela home alone. Angela doesn't mind. She loves going to her grandparents' home and looks forward to it each summer. They live on a farm and she gets to ride horses every day. This year she is going to be old enough to help on the farm and she is very excited about that.

Great Ideas for Teaching, Inc.

Instructor's Worksheet: Part 2

Directions: After the stories have been read aloud by the instructor, the students should then answer the following questions for each story. The students should look at the picture pages for visual support. The first two sets of questions review the stories while the following questions break the information into higher-level language comprehension skills. Finally, the students should retell each story, giving as many details as possible.

Story #1

Story #2

Reviewing the Story About the School Talent Show:

1. What kind of show is planned at school?
2. Are the children or parents going to be in it?
3. How are the people chosen to be in the talent show? Explain.
4. What do Victor and Ellie plan to do? Explain.
5. What do their friends think about their talent? Explain.

Reviewing the Story About School Being Out for the Summer:

1. Why do the children walk rather than take the school bus? Explain.
2. What do they carry in their backpacks?
3. Do they walk alone each day? Explain.
4. Where will the boys spend the summer? Explain.
5. Where will Angela spend the summer? Explain.

Separating the Main Ideas in the Stories:

1. Which story is about having talent? Which story is about vacation time?

Forming Conclusions:

1. How do you know that trying out for a talent show is not easy? Explain.
2. How do you know Angela's mother wants her to be safe? Explain.

Separating Subtle Information:

1. Have Victor and Ellie known each other for a long time? Explain.
2. Do you think they know much about music? Explain.
3. Do their friends think they have a lot of talent? Explain.
4. Do the friends who walk to school together like each other? Explain.
5. Are all three friends allowed to ride the bus? Explain.
6. How do you know Angela's mother thinks she is too young to stay alone?
7. Who might win a special award or a prize? Explain.
8. Why will the three friends miss each other when school is out? Explain.
9. In which story is someone excited about being old enough to do something? Explain.
10. In which story does someone need to practice doing a special thing? Explain.

Great Ideas for Teaching, Inc.

Auditory Processing of Higher-Level Language Skills

Instructor's Worksheet: Part 2

Story #1

Story #2

Predicting What Will Happen Next:

1. Who may be doing a lot of outside work this summer? Explain.
2. What will happen if people think Victor and Ellie have the best song and dance routine?

Retelling the Stories:

Retell each of the stories. Tell as many interesting details as you can remember about each story.

Instructor's Worksheet: Part 1

Before beginning, each student should be given the picture page that corresponds to the story page. The stories are to be read aloud to the students as they scan their picture pages.

The purpose of the pictures and the stories is to help students learn to interpret events, gaining an understanding of concrete and subtle social interpretations, along with grasping the main points of each event. As another event takes place (another story), the students will learn to move on in following that new event, much as they would in going from event to event in their school day. By remembering the information and separating that information in certain higher-level language skills, reflecting back on the information in the stories should help them learn to better organize information about events in their daily lives.

Story #1: Rachel loves to wear pants and shirts all the time. She never wears a dress unless it is absolutely necessary for her to do so. Her parents keep insisting that she has to learn to like wearing dresses and skirts and blouses because she is a girl and girls are supposed to wear dresses to parties. Rachel just laughs and says, "Someday I will. Someday I will." One day a special invitation came inviting everyone in the family to attend their cousin's wedding. Rachel's mother told her she must wear a dress and they needed to go shopping. They found a pretty dress in Rachel's favorite color yellow. When Rachel came home, she tried the dress on for her father to see. When she saw herself in the mirror, she said, "Hey, I do look pretty good in a dress!" Her father told her she looked beautiful in her dress but that the work shoes definitely must be replaced with pretty dress shoes. Rachel laughed and agreed with her father.

Story #2:

Ms. Smith asked the students in her class to silently read the next chapter in their history books. Her students really love their history class. They have made so many nice projects, great bulletin boards and pictures about the people they read about in history class. Ms. Smith told the students to raise their hands when they had finished reading the chapter and they would start working on their next project about what they had read. Tara was the first to finish. She finished first because she is a very fast reader. She is excited to get started on the clay model that she is making of the settlers who came to Virginia. Her best friend Betty is sitting next to her. Betty plans to make a log cabin like the ones the pilgrims lived in. She will start on her project as soon as she finishes reading the chapter.

Instructor's Worksheet: Part 2

Directions: After the stories have been read aloud by the instructor, the students should then answer the following questions for each story. The students should look at the picture pages for visual support. The first two sets of questions review the stories while the following questions break the information into higher-level language comprehension skills. Finally, the students should retell each story, giving as many details as possible.

Story #1

Story #2

Reviewing the Story About Rachel Buying a New Dress:

1. What does Rachel like to wear best?
2. What does she say when her mother tells her she needs to buy a dress?
3. Why did Rachel and her mother decide to buy a dress? Explain.
4. What color is Rachel's dress?
5. How does her dad think she looks in a dress?

Reviewing the Story About Ms. Smith's History Class:

1. What subject does Ms. Smith teach?
2. What are some of the things the students do in history class? Explain.
3. Why is Tara's hand raised? Explain.
4. What project does Tara have planned? Explain.
5. What project does her friend Betty have planned? Explain.

Separating the Main Ideas in the Stories:

1. Which story is about dressing for a special occasion?
2. Which story is about learning more about people who lived long ago?

Forming Conclusions:

1. The teacher said the students can work on their projects when they finish reading the chapter. Will the fastest readers or the slowest readers probably start their projects first? Explain.
2. Rachel bought a new dress to wear to her cousin's wedding. Is Rachel happy or sad about finally buying a dress? Explain.

Separating Subtle Information:

1. In which story are students learning information about the past?
2. In which story is being a good reader very helpful? Explain.
3. In which story does someone need to change her style of dressing? Explain.
4. In which story did someone receive a nice compliment? What was it?
5. In which story has someone been given advice? What was the advice?
6. In which story is someone eager to get started on a project? How do you know?
7. In which story did someone need to buy something special? What was it?

Great Ideas for Teaching, Inc.

Auditory Processing of Higher-Level Language Skills

Instructor's Worksheet: Part 2

Story #1

Story #2

Separating Subtle Information (continued):

8. In which story is someone happy about how she looks? Explain.
9. In which story does everyone get to select a project? Name one.
10. In which story does someone need to go shopping again tomorrow? Explain.

Predict What Will Happen Later:

1. What do you think Rachel will wear to the wedding?
2. What will the fastest readers do before the other students? Explain.

Retelling the Stories:

1. Retell each of the stories. Tell as many interesting details as you can remember about each story.

Instructor's Worksheet: Part 1

Before beginning, each student should be given the picture page that corresponds to the story page. The stories are to be read aloud to the students as they scan their picture pages.

The purpose of the pictures and the stories is to help students learn to interpret events, gaining an understanding of concrete and subtle social interpretations, along with grasping the main points of each event. As another event takes place (another story), the students will learn to move on in following that new event, much as they would in going from event to event in their school day. By remembering the information and separating that information in certain higher-level language skills, reflecting back on the information in the stories should help them learn to better organize information about events in their daily lives.

Story #1:

Sarah and Katie are at a birthday party. They are running in a race where an older child must run with a younger child. Each child has to tie one leg to the other child's leg. At the count of three, they run as fast as they can until they reach the finish line. They really need to put an arm around each other to keep their balance. Katie told Sarah not to run too fast because that will make them fall. The ones who ran fast fell down first. The ones who didn't hold on to each other also fell down. Sarah and Katie did it just right and they won the race.

Story #2:

Becky and Ken had been picking apples from the apple tree in their backyard. They noticed lots of bees around but thought the bees would leave them alone if they didn't bother the bees. That is the way bees usually acted. However, this morning the bees started swarming around them, buzzing very close to their heads. Becky said, "Let's get out of here fast. I don't think the bees want us around this morning." They started to run very fast. Only a few bees followed them and soon they stopped and flew away.

Instructor's Worksheet: Part 2

Directions: After the stories have been read aloud by the instructor, the students should then answer the following questions for each story. The students should look at the picture pages for visual support. The first two sets of questions review the stories while the following questions break the information into higher-level language comprehension skills. Finally, the students should retell each story, giving as many details as possible.

Story #1

Story #2

Reviewing the Story About a Birthday Party:

1. Describe what the partners did to get ready for the race.
2. Were the partners Sarah and Katie or Becky and Ken?
3. Why did each girl need to put one arm around the other? Explain.
4. What did Katie caution Sarah not to do? Explain.
5. Who won the race?

Reviewing the Story About Picking Apples:

1. Where was the apple tree?
2. What did Becky and Ken plan to do?
3. What were swarming near the trees?
4. What do bees usually do if you leave them alone? Explain.
5. What did Becky and Ken decide they needed to do? Explain.

Separating the Main Ideas in the Stories:

1. Which story is about running a race for fun? Which story is about running away from danger?

Forming Conclusions:

1. Sarah and Katie hoped to do well in the race by planning what they needed to do. Did their plan work out? What was the result of their good planning?
2. Becky and Ken planned to pick apples. They decided it was best to not pick apples and to run away from the bees. Do you think they made a good decision? Why?

Separating Subtle Information:

1. In which story did things go as they were planned? Explain your answer.
2. In which story did the children make a wise decision to switch plans? Explain your answer.
3. In which story were coordination and balance important? Explain.
4. In which story did quick-thinking keep the children safe? Explain.
5. In which story were the children about the same age? How do you know?
6. In which story may a prize have been given? Explain.
7. Were the people in both stories inside or outside a house? How do you know?

Instructor's Worksheet: Part 2

Story #1

Story #2

Separating Subtle Information (continued):

8. Which story had losers and winners? Explain.
9. In which story did something happen that was unexpected? Explain.
10. In which story were the children probably having more fun? Explain.

Predicting What Will Happen Next:

1. Is it likely that Sarah and Katie will do this same thing tomorrow? Explain.
2. Is it likely that Becky and Ken will attempt to pick apples again tomorrow? Explain.

Retelling the Stories:

1. Retell each of the stories. Tell as many interesting details as you can remember about each story.

Student's Page:

Story #1

Story #2

Great Ideas for Teaching, Inc.   Auditory Processing of Higher-Level Language Skills

Instructor's Worksheet: Part 1

Before beginning, each student should be given the picture page that corresponds to the story page.
The stories are to be read aloud to the students as they scan their picture pages.

The purpose of the pictures and the stories is to help students learn to interpret events, gaining an understanding of concrete and subtle social interpretations, along with grasping the main points of each event. As another event takes place (another story), the students will learn to move on in following that new event, much as they would in going from event to event in their school day. By remembering the information and separating that information in certain higher-level language skills, reflecting back on the information in the stories should help them learn to better organize information about events in their daily lives.

Story #1:

Marcy wanted to go hiking in the park with her brother Jack. He thought she was too little to be able to keep up with him but he didn't want to hurt her feelings by saying no. Marcy did keep up with him, even though she was very tired by the time they came back. Jack said, "I wish I had thought about bringing something to eat." Marcy laughed and said, "I brought a nice picnic basket. It is in the car." As they were eating, Jack said, "Marcy, you saved the day! You can hike with me anytime you want to go."

Story #2:

Marco and Ted, who are brothers, are going on a week-long camping trip with the Boy Scouts next week. They are not sure what they should pack or if their sleeping bags will be warm enough without taking an extra blanket. Marco, who is two years older than Ted, thought it might be a good idea to camp out for one night in the backyard to test their sleeping bags and to see if all of their equipment is working properly. The next morning, Ted said, "I was pretty cold. I think I should take an extra blanket." Marco agreed, "I was freezing. I am going to take a very, very warm blanket."

Instructor's Worksheet: Part 2

Directions: After the stories have been read aloud by the instructor, the students should then answer the following questions for each story. The students should look at the picture pages for visual support. The first two sets of questions review the stories while the following questions break the information into higher-level language comprehension skills. Finally, the students should retell each story, giving as many details as possible.

Story #1

Story #2

Reviewing the Story About Hiking:

1. Why did Jack think Marcy might not be able to keep up with him on the hike? Explain.
2. Why did he agree that she could come? Explain.
3. Was Marcy able to keep up with Jack?
4. What did Jack say he wished he had remembered?
5. What had Marcy done that helped them have a great day? Explain.

Review the Story About Preparing for the Camping Trip:

1. What are Marco and Ted planning to do next week? Explain.
2. What did Marco think might be a good idea? Explain.
3. Where did they pitch their tent?
4. What were they trying to find out?
5. Were either of them cold? Explain.

Separating the Main Ideas in the Stories:

1. Which story is about trying out something to see if it works? Which story is about giving someone a chance to prove what he or she can do?

Forming Conclusions:

1. Did Marcy think they might be hungry after a long hike? Did she form a correct conclusion? Explain.
2. Did Marco think it was important to find out if their sleeping bags were warm enough? After testing the sleeping bags, what else will they need to bring?

Separating Subtle Information:

1. In which story did someone test something to make sure it was all right? Explain.
2. In which story did a brother think someone was too young to go with him? Explain.
3. In which story did someone "save the day" with good thinking? Explain.
4. In which story were people going where the weather was cold? Explain.
5. In which story did two people carry out a good plan?
6. In which story did someone compliment someone for a great idea? Explain.
7. Which story took place in someone's backyard?

Great Ideas for Teaching, Inc.

Auditory Processing of Higher-Level Language Skills

Instructor's Worksheet: Part 2

Story #1   Story #2

Separating Subtle Information (continued):

8. In which story did someone set up some equipment?
9. In which story did the people do something that made them tired?
10. In which story did some of the action happen at night? Explain.

Predicting What Will Happen Next:

1. What will the campers need to add to their packing list? Why?
2. Who will not be hungry on the trip home? Why?

Retelling the Stories:

1. Retell each of the stories. Tell as many interesting details as you can remember about each story.

Instructor's Worksheet: Part 1

Before beginning, each student should be given the picture page that corresponds to the story page. The stories are to be read aloud to the students as they scan their picture pages.

The purpose of the pictures and the stories is to help students learn to interpret events, gaining an understanding of concrete and subtle social interpretations, along with grasping the main points of each event. As another event takes place (another story), the students will learn to move on in following that new event, much as they would in going from event to event in their school day. By remembering the information and separating that information in certain higher-level language skills, reflecting back on the information in the stories should help them learn to better organize information about events in their daily lives.

Story #1:

Jason broke a window today when he and his friends were playing ball. He told his dad he needed to talk to him and his dad sat down to listen to him. His dad put his hands on his shoulders and told him he was glad he told him about it and they would repair the window together. His dad knew it was an accident and that Jason felt very bad about it.

Story #2:

Peg, Wally and Bob are watching the soccer game. Peg and Bob love to watch every play but Wally just likes to talk and talk. He always misses the big plays because he is so busy talking to his friends. The score has been tied for a long time and Wally has spent most of the time complaining about the tied score. Suddenly, Peg and Bob get very excited and start clapping and cheering. Their team scored the winning goal. Peg said, "Wally, you missed the big play again! You were too busy talking." Peg could tell that Wally was disappointed that he had missed the big play.

Instructor's Worksheet: Part 2

Directions: After the stories have been read aloud by the instructor, the students should then answer the following questions for each story. The students should look at the picture pages for visual support. The first two sets of questions review the stories while the following questions break the information into higher-level language comprehension skills. Finally, the students should retell each story, giving as many details as possible.

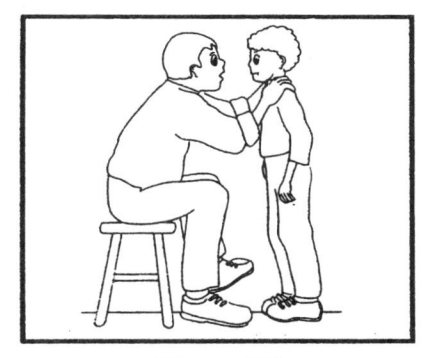

Story #1

Story #2

Reviewing the Story About Jason Telling His Father He Broke a Window:

1. What kind of accident did Jason have? Explain.
2. What did Jason dread doing? Explain.
3. Did his father yell at him?
4. Was his father glad Jason told him about it? Explain.
5. What did his father tell him they would do together? Explain.

Reviewing the Story About Peg, Wally and Bob Watching the Soccer Game:

1. What do Peg and Bob like to do when they go to a soccer game? Explain.
2. What does Wally do instead of watching the game? Explain.
3. Why does Wally never see the big plays in the game? Explain.
4. Why did Peg and Bob suddenly get excited?
5. Did Wally see their team score a goal? Why not?

Separating the Main Ideas in the Stories:

1. Which story is about an accident that happened? Which story is about someone who misses a lot because he can't stop talking?

Forming Conclusions:

1. Did Jason think his father would be able to help him solve his problem about breaking a window? Was he right? Explain how.
2. Did Peg and Bob think Wally would probably miss seeing a goal scored. Were they right? Explain.

Separating Subtle Information:

1. In which story did you hear about someone who talked too much? Explain.
2. In which story did you hear about someone who felt very bad about something? Explain.
3. In which story did you hear about someone who needed the advice of a grown person? Explain.
4. In which story did someone not pay attention to what was going on? Explain.
5. In which story did someone have an accident? Explain.
6. Did Wally miss seeing the point scored because he had an accident or because he didn't pay attention? Explain.
7. Which story was about getting excited? Explain.

Instructor's Worksheet: Part 2

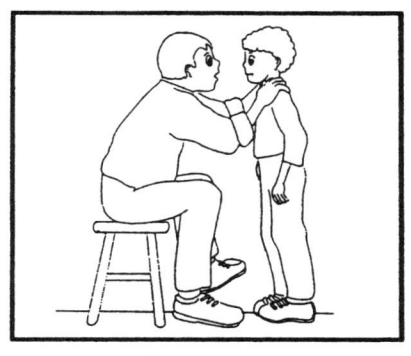

Story #1 **Story #2**

Separating Subtle Information (continued):

8. Which story is about courage and truthfulness? Explain.
9. Did Wally's talking keep the other children from watching the game? Explain.
10. Did Peg tell Wally, in a nice way, that he should watch more and talk less? Explain.

Predicting What Will Happen Next:

1. Will Jason and his dad resolve the problem of the broken window? How?
2. Do you think Wally will talk less at the next game or just keep on talking?

Retelling the Stories:

1. Retell each of the stories. Tell as many interesting details as you can remember about each story.

Instructor's Worksheet: Part 1

Before beginning, each student should be given the picture page that corresponds to the story page. The stories are to be read aloud to the students as they scan their picture pages.

The purpose of the pictures and the stories is to help students learn to interpret events, gaining an understanding of concrete and subtle social interpretations, along with grasping the main points of each event. As another event takes place (another story), the students will learn to move on in following that new event, much as they would in going from event to event in their school day. By remembering the information and separating that information in certain higher-level language skills, reflecting back on the information in the stories should help them learn to better organize information about events in their daily lives.

Story #1:

Karl is having trouble with math. He is so sad about having trouble that he just doesn't want to try anymore. His big brother Paul said, "Let me help you. Let me explain the math problems to you and you may understand them better." Paul was very patient with his brother and pretty soon Karl began to understand all of the math. He asked, "Paul, will you help me a little every day until I catch up on everything?" His brother told him he would be very glad to do that.

Story #2:

Mary and Dave went out in their backyard and sat under an apple tree while they talked about how they wanted to dress up for Halloween. Mary reached for an apple and ate it while Dave told her he wanted to be a pirate. Mary said she thought she might like to be a princess. After they finished talking about their plans, Mary said, "Let's take all the apples we can carry to mother and see if she will bake us an apple pie."

Instructor's Worksheet: Part 2

Directions: After the stories have been read aloud by the instructor, the students should then answer the following questions for each story. The students should look at the picture pages for visual support. The first two sets of questions review the stories while the following questions break the information into higher-level language comprehension skills. Finally, the students should retell each story, giving as many details as possible.

Story #1

Story #2

Reviewing the Story About Karl Having Trouble with Math:

1. Why was Karl sad? Explain.
2. Did someone offer to help him? Who?
3. Was Paul able to help Karl? How did he help him?
4. What did Karl ask his brother Paul?
5. What did Paul say?

Reviewing the Story About Mary and Dave Under the Apple Tree:

1. Where was the apple tree?
2. What were they discussing?
3. What did Dave want to be for Halloween?
4. What did Mary want to be for Halloween?
5. After they made their plans, what did Mary say to Dave?

Separating the Main Ideas in the Stories:

1. Which story is about making Halloween plans? Which story is about having big problems in math?

Forming Conclusions:

1. Did Paul think Karl was discouraged because he did not understand the math problems? Was he right? How did he help Karl?
2. Mary and Dave thought they needed to talk about what they would be for Halloween. Were they able to decide what they wanted to be?

Separating Subtle Information:

1. In which story do the children have a favorite place to talk about things? Explain.
2. In which story did someone feel like he was not very smart? Why?
3. In which story did someone feel so bad that he didn't even want to try anymore? Explain.
4. In which story did important decisions need to be made? Explain.
5. In which story do the children have something wonderful in their very own backyard?
6. In which story does someone take the time to help someone else? Explain.
7. In which story are both children young? How do you know?

Instructor's Worksheet: Part 2

Story #1

Story #2

Separating Subtle Information (continued):

8. Which story calls for good listening and good comprehension skills? Explain.
9. In which story will someone ask her mother to do something? What and why?
10. In which story was a big brother able to cheer up his younger brother?

Predicting What Will Happen Next:

1. Will Karl probably be happier in math class tomorrow? Why?
2. Will Mary and Dave probably have a nice dessert tomorrow? What will it be?

Retelling the Stories:

1. Retell each of the stories. Tell as many interesting details as you can remember about each story.

Student's Page:

Story #1

Story #2

Great Ideas for Teaching, Inc. 33 Auditory Processing of Higher-Level Language Skills

Instructor's Worksheet: Part 1

Before beginning, each student should be given the picture page that corresponds to the story page. The stories are to be read aloud to the students as they scan their picture pages.

The purpose of the pictures and the stories is to help students learn to interpret events, gaining an understanding of concrete and subtle social interpretations, along with grasping the main points of each event. As another event takes place (another story), the students will learn to move on in following that new event, much as they would in going from event to event in their school day. By remembering the information and separating that information in certain higher-level language skills, reflecting back on the information in the stories should help them learn to better organize information about events in their daily lives.

Story #1:

Tom's dad was raking leaves in the yard. Tom walked out to his dad. His dad asked, "Why Tom, have you come out to help me with the leaves?" Tom looked at his dad and said, "Uh...well, not really, Dad, I was just coming to ask you if it would be all right with you if I walked over to the ball field." Tom's dad laughed and said, "I had a feeling you were not volunteering to rake leaves." Tom told his dad he would help him if he really wanted him to. His dad said, "I'll rake these up today and then tomorrow you can rake up the leaves that fall during the night."

Story #2:

Cindy and Sid are playing together. Cindy asked Sid if he knew how to turn cartwheels and to walk on his hands. Sid said he had never tried it but it looked easy. Cindy told him it was very easy and she showed him how she walks on her hands. Sid tried it several times and each time he fell down in the grass. He told Cindy it was not as easy as it looked. She could walk on her hands as much as she wanted to, but he was going to walk on his feet.

Instructor's Worksheet: Part 2

Directions: After the stories have been read aloud by the instructor, the students should then answer the following questions for each story. The students should look at the picture pages for visual support. The first two sets of questions review the stories while the following questions break the information into higher-level language comprehension skills. Finally, the students should retell each story, giving as many details as possible.

Story #1

Story #2

Reviewing the Story About Raking Up Leaves:

1. Where was Tom's dad and what was he doing? Explain.
2. Who walked up to talk to his dad?
3. What did Tom's dad ask?
4. What did Tom say was the reason he came to talk to his dad?
5. When will it be Tom's turn to rake leaves?

Reviewing the Story About the Children Trying to Walk on Their Hands:

1. What can Cindy do that Sid cannot do?
2. Did Sid think it looked hard or easy?
3. Did Cindy say it was hard or easy?
4. What happened when Sid tried to turn cartwheels and walk on his hands? Explain.
5. What did Sid tell Cindy?

Separating the Main Ideas in the Stories:

1. Which story is about a chore that must be done? Which story is about playing in the yard?

Forming Conclusions:

1. Did Tom's dad suspect that Tom did not come out to help rake the leaves? Was he right?
2. Would it be easy to turn cartwheels and walk on your hands on your first try? Why not?

Separating Subtle Information:

1. In which story does someone have a big chore to do? Explain.
2. Did Tom go outside to ask his dad if he could help? Explain.
3. Do you think Tom's dad minded that Tom wanted to go to the ball field? Explain.
4. Will Tom have to take his turn raking leaves? Explain.
5. What clues tell you that the weather is getting cooler?
6. What clues tell you that Cindy and Sid are playing in the summer time?
7. Do you think Cindy often turns cartwheels and walks on her hands? How do your know this?
8. Did Sid find that it was harder than it looked? Explain.
9. Did he think walking on his hands was as much fun as Cindy did? Explain.
10. What did Sid decide to do after he fell a few times? Explain.

Instructor's Worksheet: Part 2

Story #1

Story #2

Predicting What Will Happen Next:

1. What will Tom's dad expect Tom to do tomorrow? Explain.
2. Does Sid plan to keep trying to do cartwheels and walking on his hands? Explain.

Retelling the Stories:

1. Retell each of the stories. Tell as many interesting details as you can remember about each story.

Instructor's Worksheet: Part 1

Before beginning, each student should be given the picture page that corresponds to the story page. The stories are to be read aloud to the students as they scan their picture pages.

The purpose of the pictures and the stories is to help students learn to interpret events, gaining an understanding of concrete and subtle social interpretations, along with grasping the main points of the event. As another event takes place (another story), the students will learn to move on in following that new event, much as they would in going from event to event in their school day. By remembering the information and separating that information in certain higher-level language skills, reflecting back on the information in the stories should help them learn to better organize information about events in their daily lives.

Story #1:

Nick was standing out in the yard. Someone shouted, "Look out!" Nick looked down and there was a snake. He let out a shout and jumped back. It scared him so badly that his heart started pounding. After he saw how small the snake was and that it was only a garden snake, he wasn't frightened anymore, but it surely gave him a scare when he first saw it.

Story #2:

Leo was sitting in the grass, taking a short rest after doing a lot of running. He started to get up again when he saw that a butterfly had landed on his sneaker and was taking a rest also. Leo sat very still, watching the butterfly. He decided that he was not going to move until the butterfly decided to fly away.

Story #3:

Millie and Doug are swimming. Doug said, "Let's have a race. I'll race you to the dock." Millie said that sounded like a great idea but that Doug must not start swimming until they were both ready and they counted to three together. Millie knows that Doug always tries to get a head start when they have a race.

Great Ideas for Teaching, Inc.

Auditory Processing of Higher-Level Language Skills

Instructor's Worksheet: Part 2

Directions: After the stories have been read aloud by the instructor, the students should complete the activities and answer the questions while looking at their picture pages for visual support. Various higher-level language comprehension skills are covered. Finally, the students should retell each story, giving as many details as possible.

Story #1   Story #2   Story #3

Remembering and Separating Story Details:

1. In which story did someone decide to sit very still? Explain.
2. In which story did someone decide to have a race? What kind?
3. In which story did someone's heart start pounding? Why?
4. In which story was an insect very close to someone? What insect?
5. In which story was someone afraid and then not afraid? Why?
6. In which story is there no mention of a snake or a butterfly?

Separating Subtle Information:

1. In which story does someone try to do better than the other person? Explain.
2. In which story does someone know that if they move, they will end what is happening? Explain.
3. In which story does someone's heart rhythm change? Explain.

Indentifying the Main Idea of Each Story:

1. Having a race.
2. Being startled and frightened.
3. Having patience.

Predicting Outcomes:

1. Story #1: The snake will be killed or the harmless little snake will slither away on the grass.
2. Story #2: Leo will sit very still and watch the butterfly for a while or Leo will jump and scare the butterfly away.
3. Story #3: Doug will cheat and start swimming before they count or Doug will wait until they count to three before he starts racing.

Finding Cause and Effect:

1. Nick jumped. (The effect.) What was the cause?
2. The butterfly didn't move. (The effect.) Why not or what caused it not to move?
3. Doug usually wins. (The effect.) Why or what causes him to usually win?

Retelling the Stories:

1. Retell each of the stories. Tell as many interesting details as you can remember about each story.

Great Ideas for Teaching, Inc.

Auditory Processing of Higher-Level Language Skills

Student's Page:

Story #1

Story #2

Story #3

Great Ideas for Teaching, Inc.

Auditory Processing of Higher-Level Language Skills

Instructor's Worksheet: Part 1

Before beginning, each student should be given the picture page that corresponds to the story page. The stories are to be read aloud to the students as they scan their picture pages.

The purpose of the pictures and the stories is to help students learn to interpret events, gaining an understanding of concrete and subtle social interpretations, along with grasping the main points of the event. As another event takes place (another story), the students will learn to move on in following that new event, much as they would in going from event to event in their school day. By remembering the information and separating that information in certain higher-level language skills, reflecting back on the information in the stories should help them learn to better organize information about events in their daily lives.

Story #1:

Betty is trying to teach her dog a new trick. She wants her dog to look in the opposite direction so it can see where she is going to throw the ball. Her dog just keeps looking at the ball even though Betty is trying to hide it behind her back. Betty is having a hard time teaching her dog to chase the ball.

Story #2:

Bill has been collecting some special rocks for his science fair. He put them in his pocket when he found them. However, he did not know he had a hole in his pocket and when he arrived home, he had no rocks. He decided the best way to find them was to walk back the same way he came home to see if he could find them. He had walked back most of the way when he heard a thud. His foot kicked something solid. When he looked down, all four of the rocks he lost were in the grass in front of him.

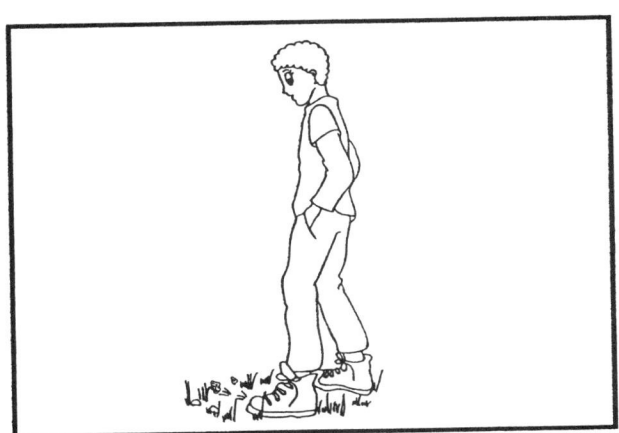

Story #3:

Little Joey had been talking to his big brother Jake ever since they started walking. Jake had not said a word. Finally, little Joey tapped his brother on the arm and asked, "Jake, are you listening to me? I don't think you have heard a word I said." Joey was right. His brother was thinking of other things and had not listened to anything Joey had told him.

Great Ideas for Teaching, Inc.

Auditory Processing of Higher-Level Language Skills

Instructor's Worksheet: Part 2

Directions: After the stories have been read aloud by the instructor, the students should complete the activities and answer the questions while looking at their picture pages for visual support. Various higher-level language comprehension skills are covered. Finally, the students should retell each story, giving as many details as possible.

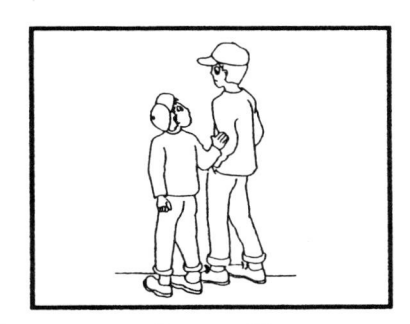

Story #1   **Story #2**   **Story #3**

Remembering and Separating Story Details:

1. In which story did someone lose something? Explain.
2. In which story is someone trying to teach her pet a game? Explain.
3. In which story is someone not listening well? Explain.
4. In which story is the pet just not understanding? Explain.
5. In which story is someone's mind on something else? How do you know?
6. In which story is someone looking for something? Why?

Separating Subtle Information:

1. In which story are the words not being understood? Why not?
2. In which story did someone decide on a good plan to find something that was lost? Explain.
3. In which story did someone "tune someone out?" Explain.

Identifying the Main Idea of Each Story:

1. Talking on and on and on.
2. Teaching tricks.
3. The hole in the pocket.

Predicting Outcomes:

1. Story #1: The dog will run after the ball or the dog will stay where the ball is.
2. Story #2: The boy will kick the rocks out of his way or the boy will pick up the rocks.
3. Story #3: The older brother will tell his little brother to be quiet or the older brother will start listening to his little brother.

Finding Cause and Effect:

1. The dog sees the girl still holding the ball (cause) so the dog _____. (effect)
2. The boy has a hole in his pocket (cause). That is why the rocks _____. (effect)
3. The little brother is talking too much (cause) and his brother is _____. (effect)

Retelling the Stories:

1. Retell each of the stories. Tell as many interesting details as you can remember about each story.

Great Ideas for Teaching, Inc.

Auditory Processing of Higher-Level Language Skills

Instructor's Worksheet: Part 1

Before beginning, each student should be given the picture page that corresponds to the story page. The stories are to be read aloud to the students as they scan their picture pages.

The purpose of the pictures and the stories is to help students learn to interpret events, gaining an understanding of concrete and subtle social interpretations, along with grasping the main points of the event. As another event takes place (another story), the students will learn to move on in following that new event, much as they would in going from event to event in their school day. By remembering the information and separating that information in certain higher-level language skills, reflecting back on the information in the stories should help them learn to better organize information about events in their daily lives.

Story #1:

Cindy decided to bake cupcakes. She thought she had put all the ingredients in her batter but when she tasted the batter, it wasn't sweet at all. She thought, "Oh, no! I forgot to put in sugar." She was so glad she had tasted the batter before she put the batter in the pans to bake.

Story #2:

Beth has been digging in the garden where she wants to plant some flowers. It was hard work and now she is sitting on the ground to rest. Her dog Spot came up and started digging in the garden. Beth asked, "What are you doing? Why are you digging that deep hole?" Then Beth saw a big bone on the grass. She knew that Spot wanted to bury the bone in her flower garden.

Story #3:

Will was watching a television program with his parents. The program was about cats. Will thought his dog would love seeing the show so he put his dog on his lap to watch. As you can see, his dog was not interested at all in seeing the cats and went to sleep.

Great Ideas for Teaching, Inc.

Auditory Processing of Higher-Level Language Skills

Instructor's Worksheet: Part 2

Directions: After the stories have been read aloud by the instructor, the students should complete the activities and answer the questions while looking at their picture pages for visual support. Various higher-level language comprehension skills are covered. Finally, the students should retell each story, giving as many details as possible.

Story #1 **Story #2** **Story #3**

Remembering and Separating Story Details:

1. In which story did someone forget something important? Explain.
2. In which story was there a program about cats? Explain.
3. In which story was something being hidden? Explain.
4. In which story is someone making something? What?
5. In which story was there something in the garden besides flowers? Explain.
6. In which story did the people enjoy something but the dog didn't? Explain.

Separating Subtle Information:

1. In which story was something almost ruined? Explain.
2. In which story was the dog very bored? Why?
3. In which story did the dog find a great spot for burying something? Why?

Identifying the Main Ideas of Each Story:

1. Digging a hole.
2. Making a cake.
3. Watching a cat show.

Predicting Outcomes:

1. Story #1: The cake will be ruined or she adds sugar and the cake will be fine.
2. Story #2: The dog will give the bone to Beth or the dog will bury the bone.
3. Story #3: The dog will bark at the cats or the dog will sleep through the whole TV show.

Finding Cause and Effect:

1. Cindy forgot to put sugar in the batter (cause) so the cake was almost _____ (effect).
2. Will thought his dog would love seeing the cats (cause) but the dog is so bored it _____ (effect).
3. Spot wants to bury a bone (cause) so he _____ in the soft dirt (effect).

Retelling the Stories:

1. Retell each of the stories. Tell as many interesting details as you can remember about each story.

Great Ideas for Teaching, Inc. Auditory Processing of Higher-Level Language Skills

Student's Page:

Story #1

Story #2

Story #3

Instructor's Worksheet: Part 1

Before beginning, each student should be given the picture page that corresponds to the story page. The stories are to be read aloud to the students as they scan their picture pages.

The purpose of the pictures and the stories is to help students learn to interpret events, gaining an understanding of concrete and subtle social interpretations, along with grasping the main points of the event. As another event takes place (another story), the students will learn to move on in following that new event, much as they would in going from event to event in their school day. By remembering the information and separating that information in certain higher-level language skills, reflecting back on the information in the stories should help them learn to better organize information about events in their daily lives.

Story #1:

Juan and Colin are playing chess. Colin is a very good player, but Juan is just learning how to play. Colin is teaching him. Colin can already tell that Juan is going to be a very good player after he learns the game. Colin is glad that he is going to have someone to play chess with when the weather gets cold and they cannot play outdoors anymore.

Story #2:

Jason picked up a little baby rabbit to hold for a minute. His dog Rusty started barking like crazy. Jason didn't know if his dog wanted to see the baby rabbit or if his dog wanted him to put the rabbit down. He told Rusty to stop barking but Rusty just barked more and more. Jason said, "I think Rusty is jealous. I need to put the baby rabbit back in its pen."

Story #3:

Ted wanted to raise a few chickens at home and have them lay fresh eggs for the family. Their house was on a big piece of property and he and his dad built a chicken coop for the chickens. Ted's dad told him not to let the chickens get out because they are such fast runners and would be hard to catch. One day, one chicken did get out when Ted opened the door of the coop. Ted chased that little chicken all over the yard until he finally caught it. His dad was right that chickens can run very, very fast.

Great Ideas for Teaching, Inc.

Auditory Processing of Higher-Level Language Skills

Instructor's Worksheet: Part 2

Directions: After the stories have been read aloud by the instructor, the students should complete the activities and answer the questions while looking at their picture pages for visual support. Various higher-level language comprehension skills are covered. Finally, the students should retell each story, giving as many details as possible.

Story #1   **Story #2**   **Story #3**

Remembering and Separating Story Details:

1. In which story was a dog upset? About what?
2. In which story was a boy chasing something? Why?
3. In which story was someone learning to play something? What?
4. In which story were friends playing together? What were they doing?
5. In what story was there a coop? What kind was it?
6. In what story was an animal being petted? Explain.

Separating Subtle Information:

1. In which story did something happen because the boy wasn't being careful? What?
2. In what story is someone planning to play chess this winter? Explain.
3. In what story is a pet jealous? Explain.

Identifying the Main Ideas of the Stories:

1. A jealous pet.
2. Teaching a game.
3. Chickens can run fast.

Predicting Outcomes:

1. Story #1: Colin will have no one to play chess with or Colin and Juan will play chess all winter.
2. Story #2: Jason will ignore Rusty and keep holding the baby rabbit or Jason will put the rabbit back in its pen and hold Rusty.
3. Story #3: Ted will let the chicken out tomorrow or Ted will be more careful when he opens the coop tomorrow.

Finding Cause and Effect:

1. Colin is teaching Juan to play chess (cause) so this winter they _____ (effect).
2. Jason is holding the baby rabbit (cause) and Rusty is _____ (effect).
3. Ted wasn't careful when he opened the coop (cause) and the chicken _____ (effect).

Retelling the Stories:

1. Retell each of the stories. Tell as many interesting details as you can remember about each story.

Great Ideas for Teaching, Inc.   Auditory Processing of Higher-Level Language Skills

Student's Page:

Story #1

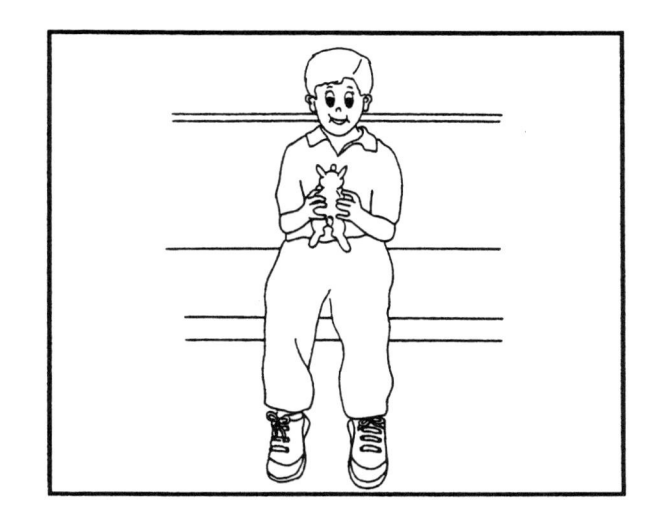

Story #2

Story #3

Great Ideas for Teaching, Inc.

Auditory Processing of Higher-Level Language Skills

Instructor's Worksheet: Part 1

Before beginning, each student should be given the picture page that corresponds to the story page. The stories are to be read aloud to the students as they scan their picture pages.

The purpose of the pictures and the stories is to help students learn to interpret events, gaining an understanding of concrete and subtle social interpretations, along with grasping the main points of the event. As another event takes place (another story), the students will learn to move on in following that new event, much as they would in going from event to event in their school day. By remembering the information and separating that information in certain higher-level language skills, reflecting back on the information in the stories should help them learn to better organize information about events in their daily lives.

Story #1:

Steve found a little rabbit in his backyard this morning. He did not see its mother and thought maybe it had wandered too far from its nest and was lost. He sat on a bench holding the little rabbit and wondering what he should do. Suddenly, he saw a big rabbit at the edge of the bushes. He told the little rabbit he thought it was its mother. He put the baby rabbit on the grass. The baby saw the mother rabbit and hopped as fast as it could to her. As quick as a flash, they both ran out of sight through the bushes.

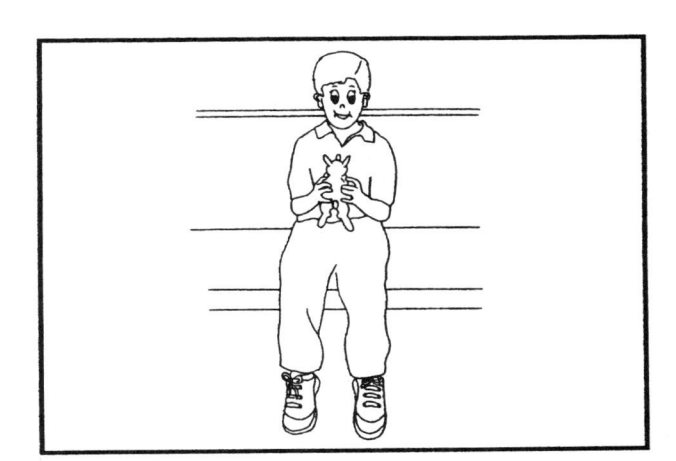

Story #2:

Bella and Lynn are on the soccer team. Their team won the state championship yesterday and today they are being honored at school. Signs have been made and put all over the school. The whole team is going to march across the soccer field and each one will be given a small trophy. They are so excited. This is going to be a wonderful day.

Story #3:

Last night Jenny told her mother that she planned to get up early the next morning so she could take a walk before breakfast. Her mother laughed and told her she was too much of a sleepy head to ever get up early. The next morning everyone was up early ready to eat breakfast when her mother asked, "Has anyone seen Jenny?" They went to Jenny's room and found her asleep in her bed.

Instructor's Worksheet: Part 2

Directions: After the stories have been read aloud by the instructor, the students should complete the activities and answer the questions while looking at their picture pages for visual support. Various higher-level language comprehension skills are covered. Finally, the students should retell each story, giving as many details as possible.

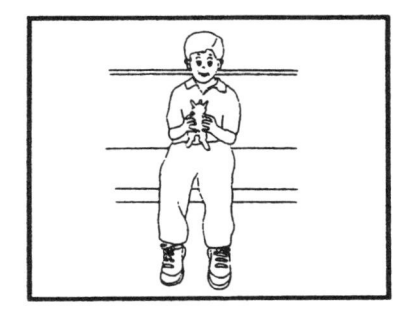

Story #1   **Story #2**   **Story #3**

Remembering and Separating Story Details:

1. In which story is someone being honored today? Explain.
2. In which story did someone have a great plan but didn't do it? Explain.
3. In which story did someone try to help a small animal? Explain.
4. In which story did someone win something special? Explain.
5. In which story did a mother look for a baby? Explain.
6. In which story was there a sleepy-head? Explain.

Separating Subtle Information:

1. In which story was a kind deed done? Explain.
2. In what story did someone not do what she said?
3. In what story is there going to be a celebration?

Identifying the Main Ideas of Each Story:

1. Sleepy-heads can't wake up.
2. Celebrating a championship.
3. Helping a baby animal.

Predicting Outcomes:

1. Story #1: The mother rabbit is not around or the mother rabbit came to find her baby.
2. Story #2: It will be a terrible day for the champions or it will be a wonderful day for them.
3. Story #3: Jenny will take her walk before breakfast or Jenny will still be sleeping when the family has breakfast.

Finding Cause and Effect:

1. Jenny overslept (cause) so she will not _____ (effect).
2. The soccer team won the state championship (cause) so the school will _____ (effect).
3. The baby rabbit saw its mother (cause) so it _____ (effect).

Retelling the Stories:

1. Retell each of the stories. Tell as many interesting details as you can remember about each story.

Instructor's Worksheet: Part 1

Before beginning, each student should be given the picture page that corresponds to the story page. The stories are to be read aloud to the students as they scan their picture pages.

The purpose of the pictures and the stories is to help students learn to interpret events, gaining an understanding of concrete and subtle social interpretations, along with grasping the main points of the event. As another event takes place (another story), the students will learn to move on in following that new event, much as they would in going from event to event in their school day. By remembering the information and separating that information in certain higher-level language skills, reflecting back on the information in the stories should help them learn to better organize information about events in their daily lives.

Story #1:

Theo has a habit of daydreaming. When he is supposed to read, he will daydream instead. When he is supposed to be writing, he will daydream instead. Theo's teacher asked, "Theo, what are we going to do to stop you from daydreaming?" Theo, who is always happy, just smiled and said, "I try to read, I try to write, but I just always seem to end up daydreaming." The teacher said, "Theo, I think I have the answer. I am going to put your desk right next to mine. That way, I can call your name every time I see you start to daydream."

Story #2:

Wilbur lives on a farm. He is still pretty young so his daily chore is to gather the eggs. He usually carries a basket for the eggs, but today he forgot the basket. Rather than go back to get the basket, he decided to carry all the eggs in his arms today. What a mistake! The eggs started slipping. When he tried to stop them from slipping, they just slipped more. It is certainly not easy to stop a round egg from slipping and rolling. Wilbur told his mom that had made a bad decision when he decided to carry the eggs and that he would never do that again.

Story #3:

Don had a dental appointment at lunch time today. His mother picked him up from school and then brought him back after the appointment. When he came back, he stopped by the cafeteria. Lunch was over but his favorite cafeteria worker told him to come on in and she would get him some lunch. What a special treat it was to get all that attention. She told him she had a special ice cream treat for him after he finished his lunch. All Don could say was, "Wow!"

Great Ideas for Teaching, Inc.

Auditory Processing of Higher-Level Language Skills

Instructor's Worksheet: Part 2

Directions: After the stories have been read aloud by the instructor, the students should complete the activities and answer the questions while looking at their picture pages for visual support. Various higher-level language comprehension skills are covered. Finally, the students should retell each story, giving as many details as possible.

Story #1 **Story #2** **Story #3**

Remembering and Separating Story Details:

1. In which story did someone get an unexpected surprise? Explain.
2. In which story did someone make a bad decision? Explain.
3. In which story did someone have trouble paying attention? Explain.
4. In which story did a person make a big mess? Explain.
5. In which story did someone do something kind for another person? Explain.
6. In which story did a teacher know how to resolve the daydreaming problem? Explain.

Separating Subtle Information:

1. In which story was a teacher clever? Explain.
2. In which story did a mess get worse and worse? Explain.
3. In which story was a school worker extra kind. Explain.

Identifying the Main Ideas of Each Story:

1. An unexpected kindness.
2. Too much daydreaming.
3. Making a big mess.

Predicting Outcomes:

1. Story #1: The teacher will help Theo stop daydreaming or Theo and his teacher will daydream together.
2. Story #2: Wilber will try to carry the eggs in his arms again tomorrow or Wilber will never forget the egg basket again.
3. Story #3: Don will be hungry all afternoon or Don will have eaten a nice lunch.

Finding Cause and Effect:

1. Theo is not getting good grades (effect) because _____ (cause).
2. Wilber dropped most of the eggs (effect) because _____ (cause).
3. The cafeteria worker fixed Don a nice lunch (effect) because _____ (cause).

Retelling the Stories:

1. Retell each of the stories. Tell as many interesting details as you can remember about each story.

Student's Page:

Story #1

Story #2

Story #3

Story #4

Instructor's Worksheet: Part 1

Before beginning, each student should be given the picture page that corresponds to the story page. The stories are to be read aloud to the students as they scan their picture pages.

The purpose of the pictures and the stories is to help students learn to interpret events, gaining an understanding of concrete and subtle social interpretations, along with grasping the main points of the event. As another event takes place (another story), the students will learn to move on in following that new event, much as they would in going from event to event in their school day. By remembering the information and separating that information in certain higher-level language skills, reflecting back on the information in the stories should help them learn to better organize information about events in their daily lives.

Story #1:

Ted's older brother Chad has been chopping a log into smaller pieces so the pieces will fit in their fireplace. Ted came out to the backyard and told his brother he would be glad to chop the last piece in two pieces and it would take him almost no time to do it. Chad smiled because he knew it would take a long time and it would be very hard to chop but Ted insisted it would be an easy job. Chad just walked away smiling. He knew Ted would find out very quickly it was not easy to chop wood.

Story #2:

Last night it snowed and Harry couldn't wait to get outside today to try his new sled. He and his dad walked over to the nearby high school because there is a steep hill in back of it. When Harry started down the hill, his new sled went very, very fast. Harry was really scared until he reached the bottom of the hill safely. He told his dad he went so fast that he felt like he was flying down the hill rather than sledding.

Story #3:

Susie is out of school for the summer. She has all day to play in her yard. She decided the first thing she wanted to do was swing on her swing with her cat Millie. Most cats would hate to swing on a swing, but not Millie. Millie loves it and dashes to get in Susie's lap every time she starts to swing.

Story #4:

Doria is in a dance recital. This is the first recital she has ever been in and she is a little bit nervous. Her dance instructor keeps telling her to look happier and to smile a little, but Doria is too scared to look happy. Her mom told her that she was going to take all the <u>happy</u> dancers out for ice cream after the recital. Doria started laughing, threw her arms out and said, "Look at me. I am a happy dancer!"

Great Ideas for Teaching, Inc.

Auditory Processing of Higher-Level Language Skills

Instructor's Worksheet: Part 2

Directions: After the stories have been read aloud by the instructor, the students should complete the activities and answer the questions while looking at their picture pages for visual support. Various higher-level language comprehension skills are covered. Finally, the students should retell each story, giving as many details as possible.

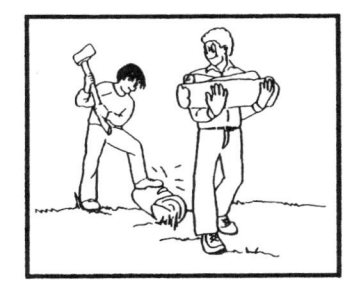

Story #1 **Story #2** **Story #3** **Story #4**

Identify the Picture of the Story that has this Information:

1. Someone was too nervous to smile. Explain.
2. Someone thinks a chore looks easy to do. Explain.
3. Someone is trying out something new. Explain.
4. Someone is celebrating summer vacation. Explain.
5. Someone decided to be happy, not nervous. Explain.
6. Someone did not expect to move so fast. Explain.
7. Someone's pet loves to swing. Explain.
8. Someone is about to find out about hard work. Explain.
9. Someone is outside in cold weather. Explain.
10. Someone's mother knew how to make her happy. Explain.

Match the Pictures to the Following Main Idea of the Stories:

1. The suddenly happy dancer.
2. It's not as easy as it looks.
3. A crazy cat can be fun.
4. Flying through the air.

Answer the "WHY" Questions:

1. Why was Harry so scared going down the hill?
2. Why couldn't Doria's mother get her to smile?
3. Why did Ted's brother walk away smiling?
4. Why is Susie's cat called "that crazy cat?"

Retelling the Stories:

1. While looking at the pictures, briefly retell each of the stories. Tell as many interesting details as you can remember about each story.

Student's Page:

Story #1

Story #2

Story #3

Story #4

Instructor's Worksheet: Part 1

Before beginning, each student should be given the picture page that corresponds to the story page. The stories are to be read aloud to the students as they scan their picture pages.

The purpose of the pictures and the stories is to help students learn to interpret events, gaining an understanding of concrete and subtle social interpretations, along with grasping the main points of the event. As another event takes place (another story), the students will learn to move on in following that new event, much as they would in going from event to event in their school day. By remembering the information and separating that information in certain higher-level language skills, reflecting back on the information in the stories should help them learn to better organize information about events in their daily lives.

Story #1:

Tim heard his friends at his front door. They were calling his name. He was upstairs in his bedroom when he heard them calling him. He leaned out the window and yelled for his friends to come on in and come upstairs to his bedroom. They are all celebrating the first day of summer vacation and plan to play basketball in Tim's driveway.

Story #2:

Maria is in the elementary school band. She is going to the middle school next year and hopes to be in the band there. She went to the middle school concert last week and they sounded so much better than the elementary school band. She decided she should practice all summer if she really, really wants to be in the middle school band.

Story #3:

Dominick wants to ride his bike over to his friend's house. His mother has already told him he has to clean his room before he can go anywhere. When he was ready to go, his mother asked him if his room had been cleaned. He told her it wasn't clean yet but he was going to do it right away. He rushed to his room, made his bed and then began to hang up his clothes. When he finished it, it had only taken him five minutes and now he was ready to go.

Story #4:

Peg is in a fitness class at school. All the children who do well in the fitness class get a certificate and are allowed to help the other students. If Peg can jump rope 100 times without stopping, this will be the last exercise she needs to complete to get the certificate. She is so excited because she knows she can easily do it.

Instructor's Worksheet: Part 2

Directions: After the stories have been read aloud by the instructor, the students should complete the activities and answer the questions while looking at their picture pages for visual support. Various higher-level language comprehension skills are covered. Finally, the students should retell each story, giving as many details as possible.

Story #1   **Story #2**   **Story #3**   **Story #4**

Identify the Picture of the Story that has this Information:

1. Someone is trying to get a special certificate. Explain.
2. Someone keeps putting off a chore. Explain.
3. Someone just started summer vacation. Explain.
4. Someone thinks she needs a lot more practice. Explain.
5. Someone is pretty confident that she can do something. Explain.
6. Someone's friends have just come. Explain.
7. Someone must do something before he can go anywhere. Explain.
8. Someone did not open the door when the guests came. Explain.
9. Someone wants to be part of a group next year. Explain.
10. Someone wants to be allowed to help other students. Explain.

Match the Pictures to the Following Main Idea of the Story:

1. Only the best players make the band.
2. Summer vacation celebration.
3. Work first, play later.
4. Earning a certificate.

Answer the "WHY" Questions:

1. Why does Peg need to jump rope 100 times without stopping?
2. Why was Dominick not allowed to ride to his friend's house?
3. Why did Tim yell to his friends?
4. Why is Maria going to play her flute every day this summer?

Retelling the Stories:

1. While looking at the pictures, briefly retell each of the stories. Tell as many interesting details as you can remember about each story.

Great Ideas for Teaching, Inc.

Auditory Processing of
Higher-Level Language Skills

Student's Page:

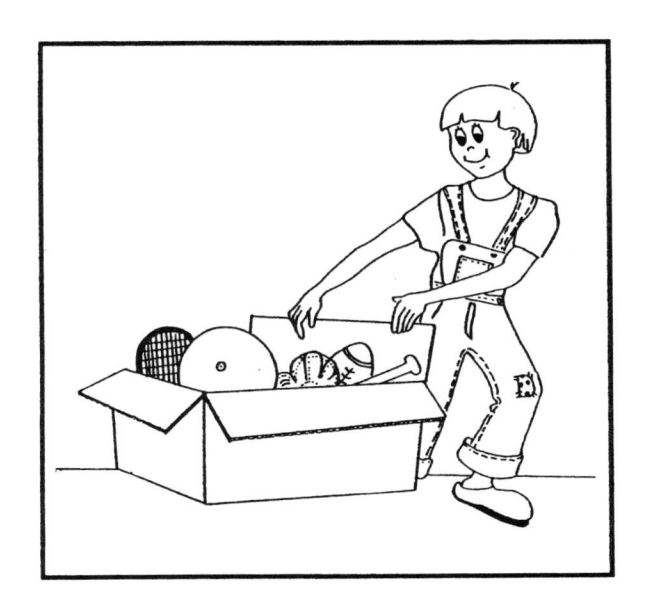

Story #1

Story #2

Story #3

Story #4

Great Ideas for Teaching, Inc.

Auditory Processing of Higher-Level Language Skills

Instructor's Worksheet: Part 1

Before beginning, each student should be given the picture page that corresponds to the story page. The stories are to be read aloud to the students as they scan their picture pages.

The purpose of the pictures and the stories is to help students learn to interpret events, gaining an understanding of concrete and subtle social interpretations, along with grasping the main points of the event. As another event takes place (another story), the students will learn to move on in following that new event, much as they would in going from event to event in their school day. By remembering the information and separating that information in certain higher-level language skills, reflecting back on the information in the stories should help them learn to better organize information about events in their daily lives.

Story #1:

Nick has been outside playing with his friends. They played football first and then they played softball. It is time to eat lunch now and everyone had to go home. Nick brought his football, softball, mitt and bat inside because he did not want them to get lost. This afternoon they are all going swimming so he knew they would not need the other things again today.

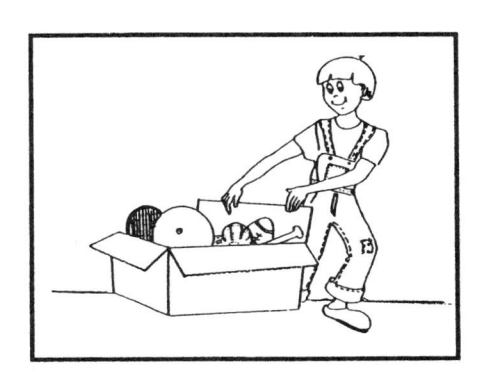

Story #2:

Jack has been to his friend's birthday party. He is just now coming home and he is so excited because he won three balloons in the games they played at the party. His mother asked him how he won the balloons and he told her he won two races and he was the only one who hit the target when they were throwing balls.

Story #3:

Melissa has a new bicycle. Her parents gave it to her for her birthday. She rides it all day long and she waves to everyone she passes. Next week, there is going to be a parade at her school. She asked her mother if she would help her decorate her bicycle so she can ride it in the parade.

Story #4:

Patrick is lying on the wooden floor reading a book. His mother saw him and asked, "Patrick, how can you be comfortable lying on that hard wooden floor?" Patrick told her he had a soft pillow under his head and that was all he needed to be comfortable. He looked comfortable and he had a nice picture hanging nearby in case he decided to rest his eyes and look at something else for a while.

Great Ideas for Teaching, Inc.

Auditory Processing of Higher-Level Language Skills

Instructor's Worksheet: Part 2

Directions: After the stories have been read aloud by the instructor, the students should complete the activities and answer the questions while looking at their picture pages for visual support. Various higher-level language comprehension skills are covered. Finally, the students should retell each story, giving as many details as possible.

Story #1   **Story #2**   **Story #3**   **Story #4**

Identify the Picture of the Story that has this Information:

1. Someone doesn't look comfortable. Explain.
2. Somone won something. Explain.
3. Someone really loves something she was given. Explain.
4. Someone is very careful with his toys and other things he owns. Explain.
5. Someone's mother is concerned about him. Explain.
6. Someone has just come back from a birthday party. Explain.
7. Someone is going swimming. Explain.
8. Someone wants to be in a parade. Explain.
9. Someone has a recent birthday. Explain.
10. Someone has come in to eat lunch. Explain.

Match the Pictures to the Following Main Idea of the Stories:

1. A favorite birthday present.
2. Learning to be responsible.
3. A three-time winner.
4. Being comfortable.

Answer the "WHY" Questions:

1. Why did Patrick's mother want him to get off the floor?
2. Why does Jack have balloons?
3. Why did Nick put away his football, softball, mitt and bat?
4. Why does Melissa want to decorate her bicycle?

Retelling the Stories:

1. While looking at the pictures, briefly retell each of the stories. Tell as many interesting details as you can remember about each story.

Student's Page:

Story #1

Story #2

Story #3

Story #4

Great Ideas for Teaching, Inc.

Auditory Processing of Higher-Level Language Skills

Instructor's Worksheet: Part 1

Before beginning, each student should be given the picture page that corresponds to the story page. The stories are to be read aloud to the students as they scan their picture pages.

The purpose of the pictures and the stories is to help students learn to interpret events, gaining an understanding of concrete and subtle social interpretations, along with grasping the main points of the event. As another event takes place (another story), the students will learn to move on in following that new event, much as they would in going from event to event in their school day. By remembering the information and separating that information in certain higher-level language skills, reflecting back on the information in the stories should help them learn to better organize information about events in their daily lives.

Story #1:

Nan is babysitting for the little boy next door. He was thirsty and Nan poured him some cold water from the refrigerator. When she started to hand it to him, his hand slipped and the cup fell to the floor, spilling all the water. The little boy was so upset that he cried. Nan told him not to cry because it was just water and the cup was not breakable and no harm was done at all. She told him to watch how easy it was to clean up and that she would get him another cup of water. She is a very nice babysitter.

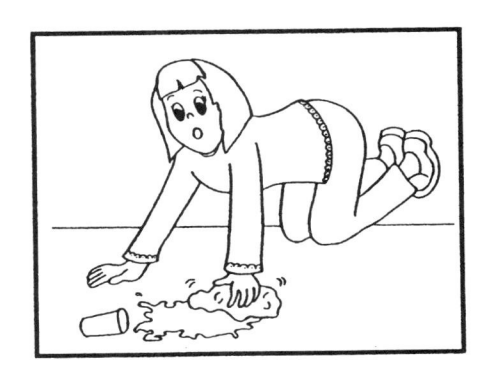

Story #2:

It is raining hard outside. Little Megan has decided to play with her doll today. She puts on a long dress-up skirt so she can play like she is a mother. She is playing house, feeding her baby doll, putting it to bed and cleaning up her play area. The phone rang. Her mother told her that her friend Susie was coming over to play dolls with her. Megan walked over to her doll and said, "Wake up, Baby, we are going to have company." Her mother laughed and said, "I think you could play house every day of the week."

Story #3:

Doug heard the phone ring and waited for someone else to answer it but no one did. After four rings, he ran to the phone and answered it. It was did dad calling from work. His dad told him someone had given him two tickets to the hockey game and his dad wanted to know if Doug would like to go. Doug was so happy he had answered the phone and not ignored the ringing.

Story #4:

Little Tommy is really sad. He has a new ball and no one to play with. He doesn't think there is much point to having a new ball if you don't have someone to play ball with. Then he remembered in a few minutes the school bus will come and all the older children will be home. Tommy will be very happy then and that sad face will have a smile on it.

Instructor's Worksheet: Part 2

Directions: After the stories have been read aloud by the instructor, the students should complete the activities and answer the questions while looking at their picture pages for visual support. Various higher-level language comprehension skills are covered. Finally, the students should retell each story, giving as many details as possible.

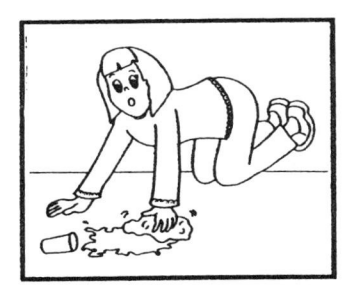

Story #1 **Story #2** **Story #3** **Story #4**

Identify the Picture of the Story that has this Information:

1. Someone had an accident. Explain.
2. Someone was lonely. Explain.
3. Someone almost missed a nice surprise. Explain.
4. Someone enjoyed playing alone. Explain.
5. Someone heard something ring. Explain.
6. Someone is babysitting. Explain.
7. Someone has something new. Explain.
8. Someone is pretending to be another person. Explain.
9. Someone is being very kind to a little child. Explain.
10. Someone is going to a sports event. Explain.

Match the Pictures to the Following Main Idea of the Stories:

1. Playing house.
2. A happy phone surprise.
3. It's just a little accident.
4. Playing alone is not fun.

Answer the "WHY" Questions:

1. Why did the little girl dress up?
2. Why was the little boy lonely?
3. Why did the boy almost miss his dad's call?
4. Why is the girl wiping up water?

Retelling the Stories:

1. While looking at the pictures, briefly retell each of the stories. Tell as many interesting details as you can remember about each story.

Great Ideas for Teaching, Inc.

Auditory Processing of Higher-Level Language Skills

Student's Page:

Story #1

Story #2

Story #3

Story #4

Great Ideas for Teaching, Inc.

Auditory Processing of
Higher-Level Language Skills

Instructor's Worksheet: Part 1

Before beginning, each student should be given the picture page that corresponds to the story page. The stories are to be read aloud to the students as they scan their picture pages.

The purpose of the pictures and the stories is to help students learn to interpret events, gaining an understanding of concrete and subtle social interpretations, along with grasping the main points of the event. As another event takes place (another story), the students will learn to move on in following that new event, much as they would in going from event to event in their school day. By remembering the information and separating that information in certain higher-level language skills, reflecting back on the information in the stories should help them learn to better organize information about events in their daily lives.

Story #1:

Ben noticed many butterflies on the flowers in his yard. Each one seemed to be different. One was a color that he had never seen before. He asked his mother for a jar so he could catch it and look at it closer. His mother did not think he could catch it but she gave him a jar anyway. Ben did catch it! He was so excited. His mom took a picture of it and then Ben set it free. It kept flying from flower to flower.

Story #2:

Abby's birthday is only a week away and no one has mentioned anything about a party. Abby thought, "I think I will write on the calendar that it is my birthday so no one will forget." She wrote ABBY'S BIRTHDAY in big letters and drew a circle around it.

Story #3:

Corky was given some bubble bath for her birthday. There were no directions on the bottle so Corky thought she should probably pour half of the bottle into her bath water. The whole bathtub filled with bubbles. Corky had never seen so many bubbles. She realized she probably should not have poured so much bubble bath in the water.

Story #4:

Carlos wants to play football and Jerry wants to play softball. They decided to pull apart a "wishbone" that had come from the chicken they had for dinner and the one who ended up with the bigger piece would decide which game they would play. They both agreed to be good sports about which game was chosen.

Great Ideas for Teaching, Inc.

Instructor's Worksheet: Part 2

Directions: After the stories have been read aloud by the instructor, the students should complete the activities and answer the questions while looking at their picture pages for visual support. Various higher-level language comprehension skills are covered. Finally, the students should retell each story, giving as many details as possible.

Story #1   **Story #2**   **Story #3**   **Story #4**

Identify the Picture of the Story that has this Information:

1. Someone is afraid that everyone will forget her birthday. Explain.
2. Someone loves to study insects. Explain.
3. Someone didn't have directions for using something. Explain.
4. Someone needs to make a decision about what to play. Explain.
5. Someone has more of something than she planned. Explain.
6. Someone wants to remind her family about a special day. Explain.
7. Someone promises to be a good sport. Explain.
8. Someone will let something fly away. Explain.
9. Someone will use less of something the next time. Explain.
10. Someone found a great way to make a decision of what to play.

Match the Pictures to the Following Main Idea of the Stories:

1. Choosing a game.
2. Reminding everyone about an important day.
3. Too many bubbles.
4. Studying insects.

Answer the "WHY" Questions:

1. Why is Abby writing on the calendar?
2. Why are the boys breaking a wishbone?
3. Why did Ben need a jar?
4. Why does Corky have so many bubbles in the bathtub?

Retelling the Stories:

1. While looking at the pictures, briefly retell each of the stories. Tell as many interesting details as you can remember about each story.

Great Ideas for Teaching, Inc.

Auditory Processing of Higher-Level Language Skills

Student's Page:

Story #1

Story #2

Story #3

Story #4

Great Ideas for Teaching, Inc.

Auditory Processing of
Higher-Level Language Skills

Instructor's Worksheet: Part 1

Before beginning, each student should be given the picture page that corresponds to the story page. The stories are to be read aloud to the students as they scan their picture pages.

The purpose of the pictures and the stories is to help students learn to interpret events, gaining an understanding of concrete and subtle social interpretations, along with grasping the main points of the event. As another event takes place (another story), the students will learn to move on in following that new event, much as they would in going from event to event in their school day. By remembering the information and separating that information in certain higher-level language skills, reflecting back on the information in the stories should help them learn to better organize information about events in their daily lives.

Story #1:

Alice's mother bought a new chair at a garage sale. She put it on the porch. Alice came home and was very, very tired. She saw the chair and decided to sit in it to rest. When she sat down, the chair leg broke and down went the chair and Alice. Alice went in the house and told her mother, "I think I know why the chair was so cheap at the garage sale."

Story #2:

Ollie couldn't find his new puppy. He wondered where the puppy was and hoped it wasn't making a mess somewhere without anyone knowing. The house was very quiet. That was not a good sign. Ollie finally found his puppy. He also found one of his best shoes with a big hole in the front of his shoe. He said, "Bad puppy!" and took the shoe away. He knew his mother was going to be very upset.

Story #3:

Maria is going to be in a gym show. She is so excited because she is the first person to perform in the show. She will come in from one side door and do flips and cartwheels across the entire stage before she goes out the other side of the stage. Every time she practices, everyone claps for her and she feels very special.

Story #4:

Cliff's dad is building a fire. He cannot get the big logs to start burning. The fire keeps going out. Cliff's dad asked Cliff if he would go outside and find some small sticks or small pieces of wood because they will catch on fire a lot quicker and then they can add the logs. Cliff found the small sticks and small pieces of wood and is bringing them to his dad.

Instructor's Worksheet: Part 2

Directions: After the stories have been read aloud by the instructor, the students should complete the activities and answer the questions while looking at their picture pages for visual support. Various higher-level language comprehension skills are covered. Finally, the students should retell each story, giving as much detail as possible.

Story #1   **Story #2**   **Story #3**   **Story #4**

Identify the Correct Story:

1. In which story did someone get sent outside to find something?
2. Who knows that a new pet must be watched closely?
3. Who knows her mother bought something new today?
4. Who is practicing for a gym show?
5. In which story was no one watching a new puppy?
6. In which story did someone have an accident?
7. In which story did someone need to find something?
8. In which story does someone have a special talent?

Correcting Incorrect Information: The students should listen to each statement and take turns correcting the information and identifying the picture for the story the information is about.

1. The girl is practicing doing cartwheels for the spring dance recital.
2. Cliff went outside to find several big logs.
3. Alice's mother bought an expensive chair today.
4. Ollie has an old dog.
5. Alice broke the chair on purpose.
6. Cliff and his dad are starting to build some shelves.
7. Maria is practicing to sing in a gym show.
8. Ollie told the puppy his dad was going to be very upset.

What is the Cause of Each Situation:

1. Why did Alice sit down in the chair?
2. Why is Ollie's mom going to be upset?
3. Why did Cliff go outside and pick up small sticks?
4. Why is Maria practicing turning cartwheels?

Retelling the Stories:

1. While looking at the pictures, briefly retell each of the four stories. Tell as many interesting details as you can remember about each story.

Student's Page:

Story #1

Story #2

Story #3

Story #4

Great Ideas for Teaching, Inc.

Auditory Processing of Higher-Level Language Skills

Instructor's Worksheet: Part 1

Before beginning, each student should be given the picture page that corresponds to the story page. The stories are to be read aloud to the students as they scan their picture pages.

The purpose of the pictures and the stories is to help students learn to interpret events, gaining an understanding of concrete and subtle social interpretations, along with grasping the main points of the event. As another event takes place (another story), the students will learn to move on in following that new event, much as they would in going from event to event in their school day. By remembering the information and separating that information in certain higher-level language skills, reflecting back on the information in the stories should help them learn to better organize information about events in their daily lives.

Story #1:

Andy is late for gym class. He knows he is not supposed to run in the hallways or on the stairs. He thinks to himself that maybe he can walk very, very fast so it will look like he is walking rather than running. He just wants to get to gym class before the bell rings.

Story #2:

Inky is the best artist in the class. Her real name is Eileen but she has been called Inky for as long as she can remember. The art teacher asked each student to draw a picture about happiness. Inky thought and thought. Suddenly she knew what she wanted to draw. She drew a big smiling sun. Inky told her teacher that happiness is a big, happy smile. Inky won the contest. All of her classmates voted for her because her picture made them happy.

Story #3:

Jimmy wants to be in the school marching band next year. He plays his trumpet very well, but he heard that each member must be a good marcher, also. He puts on music each day and practices marching to the beat of the music.

Story #4:

Ellen is trying to teach her dog to sit up and beg. Her dog kept running around and barking for the stick. After Ellen helped her dog sit up a few times, it finally understood what she wanted it to do. Now when she holds out a stick, her dog immediately sits up and begs for it. As a reward she gives it the stick and a treat.

Great Ideas for Teaching, Inc.

Auditory Processing of Higher-Level Language Skills

Instructor's Worksheet: Part 2

Directions: After the stories have been read aloud by the instructor, the students should complete the activities and answer the questions while looking at their picture pages for visual support. Various higher-level language comprehension skills are covered. Finally, the students should retell each story, giving as many details as possible.

Story #1 **Story #2** **Story #3** **Story #4**

Identify the Correct Story:

1. Who is trying to teach her pet a new trick?
2. Who knows he is not supposed to run?
3. Who must draw something that means happiness?
4. Who wants to be in the band next year?
5. Who doesn't want to be late?
6. Who wants her pet to learn something?
7. Who completed a school assignment?
8. Who wants to be in something special next year?

Correcting Incorrect Information: The students should listen to each statement and take turns correcting the information and identifying the picture for the story the information is about.

1. Ellen is trying to teach her dog to roll over.
2. Jimmy wants to be on the football team next year.
3. Andy thinks everyone is supposed to run up the stairs.
4. Inky is supposed to draw a picture about her summer vacation.
5. Jimmy plays the drums in the band.
6. Andy is running up the steps to the cafeteria to be first in line.
7. Inky is the worst artist in her class.
8. Ellen thinks her dog is too old to learn a new trick.

What is the Cause of Each of These Situations?

1. Why is Andy rushing so much?
2. Why is Jimmy practicing marching?
3. Why is Inky drawing a picture?
4. Why is Ellen holding a stick?

Retelling the Stories:

1. While looking at the pictures, briefly retell each of the stories. Tell as many interesting details as you can remember about each story.

Student's Page:

Story #1

Story #2

Story #3

Story #4

Great Ideas for Teaching, Inc.

Auditory Processing of Higher-Level Language Skills

Instructor's Worksheet: Part 1

Before beginning, each student should be given the picture page that corresponds to the story page. The stories are to be read aloud to the students as they scan their picture pages.

The purpose of the pictures and the stories is to help students learn to interpret events, gaining an understanding of concrete and subtle social interpretations, along with grasping the main points of the event. As another event takes place (another story), the students will learn to move on in following that new event, much as they would in going from event to event in their school day. By remembering the information and separating that information in certain higher-level language skills, reflecting back on the information in the stories should help them learn to better organize information about events in their daily lives.

Story #1:

Kevin has an appointment with the dentist today. He always dreads going, even though it really never hurts him and he seldom has a cavity. The dentist asked him to open his mouth. Kevin opened his mouth, but he also shut his eyes tighted and gripped the arm of the chair as tightly as he could. The dentist laughed and told him it looked he was ready to flip out of the chair and out of the room if someone pushed a button.

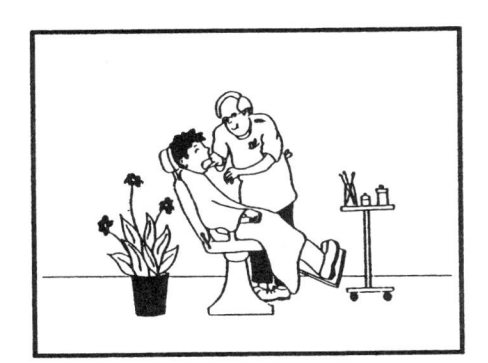

Story #2:

Katy has new roller skates. She is taking a skating class and her parents decided she needs new skates. Her toes are almost touching the front of her old skates and she needs one size larger. She told her parents that her new ones felt great. In Katy's new class, she will learn to skate backwards, to do special steps, and to dance on skates. Her best friend will be taking the class with her. When they finish the course, all the skaters will give a special skating program for their parents.

Story #3:

Sophia put on her Halloween costume and waited for her friend Tony to come to her house so they could go play Trick or Treat. The doorbell rang. Sophia is looking at someone dressed as a pig. She wonders, "Can this be my friend Tony?" Someone behind the pig mask giggles and Sophia knows it is Tony. She loves his costume.

Story #4:

Tommy lives on a farm. He loves all animals. He really likes helping his dad do all the farm chores, also. He and his dad spend a lot of time together. He just cannot imagine having a better life than living on a farm. One day, as the sheep were being rounded up, one little lamb seemed to have lost its mom. It looked so frightened. Tommy picked it up and held it in his arms. Tommy told the lamb they would just wait for the mother to come looking for her baby and soon she did head toward them.

Great Ideas for Teaching, Inc.

Auditory Processing of Higher-Level Language Skills

Instructor's Worksheet: Part 2

Directions: After the stories have been read aloud by the instructor, the students should complete the activities and answer the questions while looking at their picture pages for visual support. Various higher-level language comprehension skills are covered. Finally, the students should retell each story, giving as many details as possible.

Story #1 **Story #2** **Story #3** **Story #4**

Identify the Correct Story:

1. Who is uneasy about being where he is? Explain.
2. Who is being kind to a little animal that needs help? Explain.
3. Who is getting ready to have fun on a holiday? Explain.
4. Who is taking lessons to get better at something? Explain.
5. Who is nervous and scared? Explain.
6. Who understands a lot about farm animals. Explain.
7. Who isn't sure she knows who is behind the mask? Explain.
8. Who is going to be in a special program soon? Explain.

Correcting Incorrect Information: The students should listen to each statement and take turns correcting the information and identifying the picture for the story the information is about.

1. The boy is holding a little lost goat.
2. Sophia and her friend are going Trick or Treating for Thanksgiving.
3. Katy is taking lessons in how to play soccer better.
4. Kevin is very happy and excited about going to the dentist.
5. The mother sheep forgot all about her little lamb.
6. The dentist can tell that Kevin is very relaxed about being there.
7. Sophia can see who was in the costume.
8. Katy needed a new pair of shorts before she started skating lessons.

What is the Cause of Each of These Situations?

1. Why is Tommy holding the little lamb?
2. Why isn't Sophia really sure who is in the costume?
3. Why did Katy need new skates?
4. Why is Kevin so nervous?

Retelling the Stories:

1. While looking at the pictures, briefly retell each of the stories. Tell as many interesting details as you can remember about each story.

Great Ideas for Teaching, Inc.

Auditory Processing of Higher-Level Language Skills

Student's Page:

Story #1

Story #2

Story #3

Story #4

Instructor's Worksheet: Part 1

Before beginning, each student should be given the picture page that corresponds to the story page. The stories are to be read aloud to the students as they scan their picture pages.

The purpose of the pictures and the stories is to help students learn to interpret events, gaining an understanding of concrete and subtle social interpretations, along with grasping the main points of the event. As another event takes place (another story), the students will learn to move on in following that new event, much as they would in going from event to event in their school day. By remembering the information and separating that information in certain higher-level language skills, reflecting back on the information in the stories should help them learn to better organize information about events in their daily lives.

Story #1:

Violet's dog was digging in the trash can when Violet found it. Violet scolded her pet and told the little puppy that it smelled terrible, just like the garbage. Her puppy looked so sad. Violet filled a tub with water and gave the puppy a nice bath. The puppy was so happy that the terrible smell was gone and everyone will like holding it again.

Story #2:

Sunny and her brother Leo were hiking with their parents. They thought it would be fun to leave the trail and walk over the next hill and meet their parents on the other side. They were sure they would get there first by taking a shortcut over the hill. To their surprise, they found the ground full of rocks, ditches and dirt mounds. Sunny told her brother she thought they had made a mistake and it would take them twice as long as walking on the trail. She was right. When they reached the top of the hill, their parents were already on the other side, sitting by the road waiting for them.

Story #3:

Cindy and her dog wanted to go fishing. They are going to fish in the small pond behind Cindy's house. Cindy always wears a life jacket when they go fishing. Her dog is a super swimmer and doesn't need a life jacket. A fish leaped out of the water trying to get the worm on the hook. Cindy laughed and said, "I have a feeling this will be a great day to fish because the fish seem to be very hungry."

Story #4:

Tommy is visiting a farm with his school class. He hasn't been on a farm before and doesn't know much about farm animals. The children were told they could pet the animals but Tommy didn't listen and decided to try to ride on the back of one of the pigs. He scared the pig so badly that the pig started running and dumped Tommy off of its back into a mud puddle.

Great Ideas for Teaching, Inc.

Auditory Processing of Higher-Level Language Skills

Instructor's Worksheet: Part 2

Directions: After the stories have been read aloud by the instructor, the students should complete the activities and answer the questions while looking at their picture pages for visual support. Various higher-level language comprehension skills are covered. Finally, the students should retell each story, giving as much detail as possible.

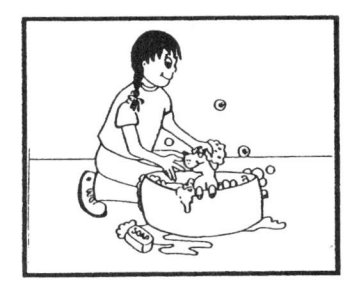

Story #1 **Story #2** **Story #3** **Story #4**

Identify the Correct Story:

1. Who is hiking today?
2. Whose dog was digging in something with a bad odor?
3. Who did something he should not have done?
4. Who loves to fish?
5. Who wanted to take a short-cut?
6. What seems to be hungry?
7. Who scared an animal?
8. Whose dog likes to be clean?

Correcting Incorrect Information: The students should listen to each statement and take turns correcting the information and identifying the picture for the story the information is about.

1. Cindy and her little dog are fishing in the ocean.
2. Sunny and Leo are hiking near the beach.
3. Violet's dog was playing in the mud.
4. Tommy only petted the pig.
5. Violet is washing her dog because he likes to take a bubble bath.
6. Cindy plans to catch the fish with cookie dough as bait.
7. Sunny and Leo plan worked for they arrived first.
8. Tommy stayed nice and clean.

What is the Cause of Each of These Situations?

1. Why did Tommy get dirty?
2. Why are Cindy and her dog in a canoe?
3. Why did Sunny and her brother take a shortcut?
4. Why is Violet giving her dog a bath?

Retelling the Stories:

1. While looking at the pictures, briefly retell each of the stories. Tell as many interesting details as you can remember about each story.